B
DROME

BLUE JELLYFISH SYNDROME

By Karen Unrue

HOW TO BREAK FREE FROM STIGMA
AND
MAINTAIN HOPE WHILE LIVING WITH A
MENTAL ILLNESS

A "TILTED ROOM" BOOK

Print Edition
ISBN: 978-0-620-75781-2

Professional typesetting by www.MYeBook.co.za

WHAT IS BLUE JELLYFISH SYNDROME?

Blue jellyfish syndrome is what a client of mine with Borderline Personality Disorder chose, at my suggestion, to call her diagnosis. She was horrified at having been given the label Borderline Personality Disorder by her psychiatrist. It made her feel abnormal, strange and scary. It made her feel stigmatized. So, while we worked together, we never again referred to her diagnosis as BPD but instead, called it blue jellyfish syndrome. She didn't mind, in the least, being a blue jellyfish. We are not our labels.

HOW TO USE THIS BOOK

Welcome dear reader,
You are free to read this book any way you like; in the bath, standing on your head, or waiting for the number 7 bus. I suggest, however, that you read it all the way through first and then use it to dip into whenever you like. That is what I had in mind when I wrote it and I believe you will get the most out of it that way.

CHAPTERS

What is blue jellyfish syndrome? v

How to use this book vii

About the author xiii

My Story xv

1. Stigma. What is it and why do I need to know about it? 1

2. Why don't people understand what I'm going through? 5

3. Why do I have a low opinion of myself and what can I do about it? 11

4. Self-talk. Is mine toxic or healthy? 19

5. How do I maintain hope? 25

6. A few final words 29

This book is dedicated to LKV

ABOUT ME

I live in England, where Queens sit on thrones, the weather is abysmal and a cup of tea solves everything. I have worked for the last 16 years as a mental health mentor and trainer for London-based charities. I also see clients privately. My passion is working with people who have lost their sense of self-worth, through abuse or life circumstances and helping them learn to love themselves and the life they live. I have experienced trauma myself and know what it is to have had crippling low self-esteem. In this book, I share with you some of the information and advice that has helped me find and maintain the most important resource there is for managing a life lived with mental illness:

HOPE

HOPE IS THE VITAL INGREDIENT IN THE CAKE MIX OF RECOVERY

MY STORY

All of us who experience mental health issues have our stories.
The following story happens to be mine.

I was floating peacefully in amniotic fluid busily growing fingers and toes when, all of a sudden, I experienced an explosive event. My mother, unaware she was pregnant and experiencing deep depression, received the first of several sessions of electric shock therapy. I can only imagine the impact that must have had on embryonic me; quite frankly, I'm surprised I wasn't born with a super power. This electric event was my introduction to the existence of mental illness and the beginning of a childhood in which I was exposed to the trauma of my mother's bi-polar roller coaster ride.

My parents loved me but their method of trying to shield me from her bouts of depression was, let's say, unhelpful; they explained nothing. When an episode of depression occurred, I saw my mother weep, watched her wring her hands, felt her disinterest in me and listened to her howl in the night hours; all distressing symptoms that were usually followed by a long disappearance. I was simply told, "mum's not very well". Only in my mid-teens did I learn that the disappearances were weeks she spent in a

Psychiatric Hospital. All I knew at the time was that my fun loving and doting mother would, to all intents and purposes, utterly abandon me. It was terrifying.

If this wasn't traumatic enough, further distress ensued because my parents belonged to a fundamentalist, evangelical Pentecostal church. It was a denomination which, in the 1970's, didn't acknowledge the existence of mental illness but instead, taught that "depression" was an affliction that people brought upon themselves, owing to a "lack of faith". Church doctrine stated that having a "lack of faith" or shock/horror, "committing a sin" (a sin being anything from smoking the occasional cigarette to bestiality), created a chink in your spiritual armour. The consequence of this was that you forfeited God's protection and demons could flood in and cause you mental distress. In other words, the teaching was that my mother herself was responsible for the reoccurring episodes of mental torment she experienced.

This repugnant belief resulted in several church elders coming to the house one Saturday afternoon and putting my poor mother through a loud and scary exorcism, as I listened outside the closed living room door. I was horrified. The necessity for such an act was apparently because God, being holy, could not coexist with sin. Therefore, if my mother wanted to heal and again, live under His protection, her sin had to be cast out. It will come as no surprise to you that her depression continued unabated.

Having witnessed the harsh consequences of God's wrath should he be displeased, I still heard preached from the pulpit every Sunday, that God loved us with such a passion that he sent his only son to die on the cross for us, so we could escape eternal damnation. It was all very confusing; a God that loved me deeply but who would, if I wasn't pleasing enough, abandon me to some unspeakable horror? I no longer hold these beliefs but at the time I didn't question them. I was a fervent believer. I loved God and was terrified. This harmful religious conditioning coupled with the regular periods of my mother's unexplained "abandonment" led me to begin to fear that neither my present, nor eternal safety, was assured. I became convinced that security was utterly dependent upon my never pissing off God. I wasn't exactly sure how you went about doing that but I was certain that if I didn't manage it, I risked abandonment and abandonment meant one thing to me – sheer terror.

There was little to indicate that I was in the process of developing an unhealthy pattern of conditioned beliefs that were to cause me lifelong damage. As a teenager, I was outgoing, confident, enjoyed strong friendships and received high grades. For the most part, the great white shark of my emerging mental illness swam submerged in my psyche. Only now and then did a fin break the surface and the abstract terror that was to become such a regular feature of my adult life would fleetingly show me its teeth. It did not occur to my loving but religious parents that these episodes of fear and anxiety warranted a visit to a qualified therapist. I was instead, taken to the pastor or a church elder, who "laid hands" on me and noisily cast out the "spirit of fear" (anything to do with demons required a lot of shouting and led me to wonder if they were hard of hearing). Once it was over, I was warned to stay closer to God. So, rather than freeing me from fear, the procedure further confirmed my belief that if I was to remain safe, I had to stay in God's good books. I stepped up my devotion and followed the rules with greater urgency.

Little wonder then that by my late teens, the shark I had previously only caught the occasional glimpse of, was breaking the surface more often. Convinced that the fears I was experiencing were of a spiritual nature, I sought only spiritual solutions. I recognise now that I was developing serious mental health issues; issues that would soon lead me to make a terrible decision. Several American airmen began attending our church from the nearby airbase when I was 19 and one of them took an interest in me. I enjoyed spending time with him and we became friends, at least I thought we were just friends. To my surprise, after only a few weeks, he proposed. I explained that I didn't think of him in that way at all and was not physically attracted to him. He seemed unfazed by my statement and we continued the friendship.

Five months later, however, we were married and on a plane travelling to his new posting in New York. I still didn't love him or find him physically attractive, so what on earth was going on? I had lived a very sheltered life and the church impressed upon us teenagers that dating non-Christians was a sin. Moreover, I attended an all-girls school, so, the only Christian boys I knew were the spotty, chinless wonders at my church youth group, none of whom I would have touched with a barge pole. This American was the first man with whom I had spent any real time. I was naïve and trusting. It didn't occur to me for a moment that someone would use God as a manipulative tool to his get what he wanted and having had no experience with men, I didn't have the slightest clue that beneath his Southern American charm, there lurked an abuser.

Following his rejected proposal, he became more attentive. He bought me expensive gifts and wined and dined me at posh venues. He continued to ask me to marry him and I continued to turn him down. Then one day he arrived at my house, very excited and said he had something wonderful to tell me. He stated that God had spoken to him, saying it was His will that we marry and work together for His Kingdom. Now I was confused. How could God have said that when he must know, I didn't love this man? I was silent for a long time and eventually responded that I wasn't sure getting married was the right thing to do because I was not in love with him. My future husband then spoke the words that, I realise now, he had carefully figured out would be the hook to catch me.

"Karen, do you want to risk not 'being pleasing' to God? Do you want to pay the price for living outside of God's will?".

It worked. All my fear-filled issues around safety and abandonment if I were not pleasing to God, flooded in. The shark was now no longer playing hide and seek with me; this man had intentionally placed me in its jaws. I agreed to marry him but only because I was too afraid of God to say no. I made sense of it by assuming God must be requiring this sacrifice of me to prove my devotion to Him. I didn't love this man but I told myself that at least I would be safe with him because I would be obeying God. I had no idea that the person in front of me, who was claiming his undying love for me, was going to put me through 10 years of mental, emotional and physical abuse.

The domestic violence I went on to experience, along with the conditioning of my upbringing, have caused my life to be interrupted for decades by periods of anxiety, episodes of depression, and several terror-filled nervous breakdowns. I have been on various medications but in 2015, I finally received the diagnosis of complex PTSD, which has led to better-directed therapy. Over the last 30 years, with grit and determination, I have come a long way and now, with a great therapist, I live my life on a much more even keel. In the following chapters, I am going to share with you some information and advice that have helped me gradually make the transition from being someone regularly paralysed by fear and low self-esteem, to someone who loves herself and the life she lives. Learning how to develop and maintain hope has been a big part of that and as you will see, it's a theme that runs through the book.

CHAPTER ONE

STIGMA. WHAT IS IT AND WHY DO I NEED TO KNOW ABOUT IT?

The Oxford dictionary defines it as,

> "A mark of disgrace associated with a particular circumstance, quality, or person."

All kinds of people find themselves at the sharp end of stigma: –

1. The physically disabled
2. Those of different ethnic origin
3. Gays, lesbians and transgender people
4. People with mental illness

Stigma expresses itself in many ways: –

1. Finger pointing and people staring.
2. Exclusion.
3. Mocking comments and laughter.
4. Rude, offensive comments and foul language.
5. Physical violence.

Such behaviour stems from ignorance, a lack of empathy, fear, or extreme judgemental beliefs.

Stigma is not a new phenomenon.

As recently as a hundred years ago, someone with epilepsy would be considered possessed by an evil spirit and a person with a cleft lip thought to have been touched by the devil. Such superstition and stigma no longer exist regarding physical conditions as there is more understanding of how the body works.

However, most people today remain ill-informed about mental illness and so stigma is attached to it.

Stigma can create an obstacle to our recovery

1. It is toxic and makes those of us with mental health issues feel ashamed, inferior and a burden. The stigma externally directed toward us is cruel and hurtful and can make us isolated and depressed.
2. We also tend to internalise stigma, which means that we come to believe the negativity we hear aimed at us to be the truth about who we are. It is very damaging as it can lead to self-loathing and hopelessness.

Those of us who have known periods of not being able to work because of mental illness, will have experienced the humiliating assessment process instigated by a government that resents spending money on the welfare system. The implication is that we are lazy scroungers who don't want to work and are often told to, "pull yourself together." Our society measures success by material means and outward signs of achievement. It is understandable, then, that we are made to feel like we have fallen short of the life we "should be living" and to see ourselves as inferior. Such attitudes create in us feelings of shame and worthlessness, which are enemies of hope.

WHAT CAN BE DONE ABOUT IT?

In the following chapters, I will help you understand how you can begin to find hope and maintain it by chipping away at the stigma you've internalised. You will come to realise you **are** of value and **not** the person stigma has led you to think you are. I will show you how you can work toward recovery and live a fuller, more enjoyable life. It's not a quick fix, there are no magic wands here but with perseverance and support, you can make it.

THERE IS HOPE.

CHAPTER TWO

WHY DON'T PEOPLE UNDERSTAND WHAT I'M GOING THROUGH?

Imagine you're involved in a car crash.

What happens next?

The medical services rush into action. Onlookers get involved in helping and comforting you until they arrive. Once in the hospital, you are assessed and treated for serious injuries, taken care of immediately by specialists and put in a bed on a ward. Family, friends, colleagues, even acquaintances visit you, send cards, flowers and maybe, even dancing girls if you're lucky. They ask you about what happened and say how glad they are you survived such an awful experience. Some will even promise to support you through the process of recovery.

Now imagine you have an emotional car crash. You are reacting to the pain of past abuse, a current situation, or a genetic condition.

What happens next?

It's very unlikely onlookers will get involved. Medical services will step in but the mental health system is so underfunded, it could take months for you get a proper assessment, a psychiatrist appointment and some talking therapy. Instead, a general practitioner will give you tranquillisers or anti-depressants then put you on a long waiting list for the treatment you desperately need and send you home.

If you're lucky and you are immediately assessed and given a bed on a psychiatric ward, it is unlikely that friends, colleagues and acquaintances will come to visit. It doesn't mean they don't care but because of the stigma surrounding mental illness, they are afraid. Some will even be judgemental of what they don't understand. You may get cards and flowers but probably no one will ask about your trauma, your pain, or promise to support you through your recovery process. It's just too far out of their comfort zone. Hopefully, close family members will stand by you but other than that, you will probably be left to cope alone.

WHY THE DIFFERENT RESPONSES?

There is no stigma attached to physical injuries. The wounds incurred in a car crash are clearly visible and people understand enough about the body that they are not afraid to draw close and support you. They may even applaud your courage as you endure your suffering.

There **IS** stigma attached to mental illness. The wounds from an emotional car crash are **invisible**; there are no physical signs of your inner pain. Most people don't know how the mind works and are afraid of the change they see in your behaviour. Trying to articulate to others what it's like to live with a mental health issue when they have not experienced it themselves is like trying to describe what swimming feels like to someone who has never been in the water.

It is painful when friends and family who don't understand distance themselves from us. It is especially hard when they go one step further and say things like, "you are attention seeking", "it's all in your head" and "you just need to pull yourself together." The sense of misunderstanding and rejection can be crushing.

It doesn't help that often we will look like there is nothing wrong with us. Furthermore, if we are managing to hold onto a job and leave the house each morning suited and booted, we will not appear to be someone who struggles each day, finding the courage of a gladiator to combat our anxieties, fears and other distressing symptoms. Other people's opinions of us distort how we think about ourselves, making us feel like we're not good enough, that maybe we ARE just lazy and unwilling to pull ourselves together. This self-doubt leaves us feeling frustrated, alone and hopeless.

I have experienced it myself

A PTSD trigger led to a nervous breakdown. I lost the job I loved and had to go on welfare. I was devastated that once again, mental illness had interrupted my life, thwarting my plans and dreams. A very close friend of mine, someone I had expected would support me, instead, turned to me and accused me of enjoying the "**pay-off**" of having mental health issues. I was shocked. I asked her what she meant. She said,

"You get to stay at home and do nothing while relying on other people to look after you financially."

Thankfully, I had by this time, come to understand the stigma surrounding mental illness and didn't buckle under her comment. I was angry and hurt but I stayed calm and replied to her,

"There is no point in me trying to articulate to you what it is like to live with my past, my wounds, my pain. I can tell you, though, that if you had to live in my mind and body for one week and experience the struggle, frustration, determination, inner resilience and courage it takes to be me, I don't think you'd cope".

What can we do about the fact that most people will not understand what we are experiencing?

ADVICE THAT HELPED ME

The battles and wounds of mental illness are invisible and not recognised by most people. We, therefore, underestimate the pain we endure every day and an internalised stigma CD plays in our heads telling us we are lazy, a burden and stupid because we can't just shake off our symptoms. I came up with an exercise that has enabled to me break that destructive pattern of thinking and I did it every time I experienced this sense of stigma. I practised it daily and over time, it has helped me and the clients I have shared it with, to have a more positive attitude towards ourselves.

THE EXERCISE

1. Close your eyes and imagine that every instance of mental cruelty, emotional abuse and trauma you have endured, all the psychological injuries you carry, are no longer invisible but can be seen on your body. Visualise them however you like; burns, bruises, bullet wounds, knife wounds, broken bones, scars.
2. Then imagine how differently you would feel about yourself because you and others could see that you had not been making it up; that your pain, your struggle, is real. You would probably be kinder to, and more patient with, yourself. Your self-esteem would improve.
3. Then think about how differently others would treat you once they could see the reality of what you live with every day. They could no longer deny your struggle is real.

This exercise, of course, doesn't enable others to see our damage but it DOES allow us to recognise that our wounds are as real as physical ones, that we have been very beaten up by life and deserve to be kinder to ourselves.

IF PEOPLE COULD SEE ON THE OUTSIDE THE BATTLES WE FIGHT ON THE INSIDE, THEY WOULD RECOGNISE US FOR THE WARRIORS THAT WE ARE!!

I also recommend spending time with others who fight invisible mental battles. It is empowering to share experiences, be understood and know you are not alone. There are lots of local support groups and charities where you can participate in enjoyable activities, sit in on informative, encouraging training sessions, or sit and chat with staff and other participants. Type mental health charities into the search engine of your computer, and you will see what is available in your area.

IT BUILDS HOPE.

CHAPTER THREE

WHY DO I HAVE A LOW OPINION OF MYSELF AND IS THERE ANYTHING I CAN I DO ABOUT IT?

Picture this scene. You have been to the supermarket and bought cream cheese and chives flavoured crisps/chips (my favourite by the way) but when opened, you find they are prawn cocktail flavour (which I can't stand). You check the label again and yes, it clearly says, "cream cheese and chives." Something is wrong and you are understandably angry.

Where do you direct that anger?

1. Do you blame the contents of the bag?
2. Do you blame the bag?
3. Do you blame the label on the bag?

No, of course, you don't.

So where does the blame belong?

Without a doubt, the person to blame is the guy who mislabelled the bag. You had no control over who was assigned to do the labelling. He might have been a nice guy having a bad day who made a mistake; he also might have been a nasty piece of work who purposefully mislabelled the product to spoil your day. Either way, what you ended up with was a label that misrepresented the contents of the bag.

You're probably thinking, "why on earth is she talking about crisps/chips"?

It's actually a useful way to illustrate a fundamental reason why we feel the way we do about ourselves.

For example –

- We all arrive in this world with no awareness of our content. We start out on this planet just like a bag of crisps/chips that has yet to be labelled.
- Our label is blank and the way we form an opinion about our contents is by reading what gets written on the label; just like a bag of crisps/chips.
- In the same way as we have no control over who labels our bag, we have no control over who our parents will be and they are the people who will be writing on our labels.

It's a genetic lottery. Here's why:

A. We could be born to well adjusted, nurturing parents who understand how to raise kids with a healthy sense of self and so they write on our label words like, "you are lovable", "you are capable" and "we enjoy your company".

B. We could be born to parents who, though well intentioned, were not well parented themselves and have no idea how to nurture a child. So, sometimes they write words on our label like, "you're a nuisance", "you're more trouble than you're worth" and "just shut up".

C. We could be born to parents who are intentionally abusive and purposefully scribble on our label words like, "you're stupid", "I wish you'd never been born" and "you'll never amount to anything".

The information we grow up reading on our labels is fundamental to the development of our mental health. It determines how we think about ourselves and whether we believe we are of value or not. How people label us in childhood, will be what we believe to be the truth of who we are.

When WE are labelled wrongly who do we blame?

Do we blame the person who did the labelling like we did with the crisp/chips bag?

NO.

- We blame the bag = ourselves
- We blame the contents of the bag = ourselves

I'm not talking about blame, so you will start hating your parents or other significant caregivers in your young life. I'm talking about blame to make you aware of the process so that you will:

STOP BLAMING YOURSELF.

WHY DOES MISLABELLING STILL AFFECT ME AS AN ADULT?

As adults, we have the capacity to think laterally. An example would be that if a friend turned up for a coffee date in a foul mood and said something like "God, you are always so damn punctual". You would not assume that she no longer liked you but would wonder what had happened to have put her in such a bad mood. You would not automatically take it personally.

Child psychologists tell us that until children are about 15/16 years old, they are incapable of lateral thinking but instead have what is called, "concrete thinking." An example would be that if a friend showed up for a play date with Stevie in a foul mood and said something like, "you're weird". Stevie would immediately take it personally and believe it to be the truth of what his friend thought of him because he isn't yet equipped to wonder what has put his good friend in a bad mood and made him behave out of character.

It is this "concrete thinking" that causes us to believe that what our caregivers have said to us and how they have treated us in our youth, is the truth of who we are. Psychologists call this "concrete thinking" because it doesn't blow away like a feather once we leave home, freeing us from its influence. No, it's hard and has set deep within us. The way it makes us feel and what it makes us believe about ourselves continues into adulthood and goes on to influence how we live our lives.

The fact that we didn't know to place the blame for this mislabelling where it rightly belonged means we believed it to be the truth about us. Do you have any idea how many successful people are driven to achieve because they are trying to prove a parent wrong about what's written on their label, so they can earn his/her approval? Equally, there are countless people whose opinion of themselves is so damaged that they have given up on life, on dreams, on themselves, have lost hope and battle with depression and anxiety.

Internalised stigma can also occur later in life, even if we have grown up in nurturing families. Bullying at work or in abusive romantic relationships can detrimentally influence our opinion of ourselves if we don't place the blame where it belongs.

I grew up in a loving but very dysfunctional family. Maybe you did too, or perhaps you had the misfortune of growing up in a purposefully abusive family. Either way, "concrete thinking" conditions us to believe the negative things written on our labels.

IS THAT IT?

Do we now have to just live with low self-esteem and how it impacts our lives?

NO

WE CAN CHANGE OUR OPINION OF OURSELVES

LET ME EXPLAIN

1. **OPINION NOT FACT**

When someone says something unkind to us, it is usually an opinion **NOT** a fact.

(There are exceptions, for instance, when my teenage son never bothered to do his homework and his teacher said he was lazy. This was a fact supported by evidence.)

I'm referring to **abusive negativity**. For instance, when a child tries to show his mother a drawing he's done and she screams at him that he is nothing but a nuisance who is always in her way. That is not a fact about him, that is her opinion; an opinion usually expressed because of some stress or worry in that mother's life. She may be stressed about finances, had a row with her husband, or not be feeling well. Her problems do not excuse the outburst but it is NOT a fact, rather an opinion voiced out of her issues.

Let me say that again.

It is NOT a fact but an opinion voiced out of some issue the parent is experiencing.

Here is a case study that illustrates my point.

STEVEN'S STORY

Steven was a good looking young man in his twenties with a steady job. He started seeing me as a client because he was depressed and beginning to think life wasn't worth living. Wanting to settle down but unable to keep a girlfriend for more than a few months, he was frustrated; women all eventually complained he was over-protective and smothering. He had even noticed his mates had begun to leave him out of events, stating similar reasons. He didn't understand why he was like this and couldn't seem to change. He had low self-esteem; in fact, he was feeling self-loathing.

In one of our sessions, I talked about how negative statements made to us by our parents when we are growing up are not always facts but are often opinions voiced out of some issue they were having. His face changed expression and he looked at me wide eyed. I asked him what light bulb moment he was having?

He related to me an incident that occurred when he was seven years old. His mother had tucked him into bed and gone downstairs to the living room, which was directly below his bedroom. Immediately, he could hear his parents arguing. It was not unusual but that evening the argument went on and on and sounded like world war three. He became scared, so he went downstairs and stood outside the closed living room door. Suddenly, the door burst open, his mother saw him standing there, pointed her finger at him and screamed,

"It's because of you that I have to stay in this marriage; it's your fault I'm so unhappy".

His light bulb moment was that he realised it was following that incident that he began to believe he was responsible for his mother's happiness. He had taken her words to be a fact about him and become hyper-vigilant, constantly concerned that if his mother wasn't ok, it must be his fault. This "truth" written on his label had deeply affected his sense of who he was and determined his behaviour into adulthood. He recognised he had been smothering and overprotective with his girlfriends and his mates because he believed he was responsible for whether anyone in his circle was happy or not.

For months, we worked together on how he could learn to live free from that "opinion" his mother had screamed at him; her mislabelling of his contents. A year or so after we completed therapy, I bumped into him at a local restaurant. He had a huge smile on his face and introduced me to his girlfriend of many months. He expressed how happy he was as he continued to practice living free from the "opinions", stated as "facts" that had caused his damaging habitual behaviour.

There is Hope of living a life free from the "opinions" that have created our low self-esteem and self-defeating behaviour.

CHAPTER FOUR

SELF TALK

Self-talk doesn't always mean the random mumblings of a drunk at the bus station. In this case, it means the chattering that goes on in our heads without us realising it most of the time. It's also called inner dialogue. The kind of inner dialogue we experience indicates what opinion we have of ourselves.

EXAMPLE

You receive an invitation to a party.

The self-talk response of someone with healthy self-esteem would sound like this:

"Great, I get to wear that new outfit. I wonder what kind of interesting people I'll meet there".

The self-talk response of someone with low self-esteem would sound like this:

"Damn, I have nothing decent to wear, probably no one will talk to me and I'll end up sitting on my own feeling awkward. I'm not going to go".

SOUND FAMILIAR?

Our self-talk reflects what is written on our labels. It also determines how we live our lives. Positive labelling makes us feel confident, free to explore new experiences and participate socially. Negative labelling means we will talk ourselves out of jobs, relationships and experiences because we believe we will fail or don't deserve them.

Are you tired of being a bystander in life more than a participant because your self-talk holds you back?

ADVICE THAT HAS HELPED ME

1. To remind myself that the negative ideas I have believed to be "facts" about me were just the "opinions" of my caregivers who spoke out of the issues they were experiencing. I don't have to own them. They are not the truth about me.
2. To remind myself I am free to think healthier thoughts about myself.
3. To **START TO BE AWARE** of my negative self-talk, remember where it comes from and challenge it each time I become aware of it.
4. To ask myself whether the negative self-talk I aim at myself is something I would say to a friend? Then choose to speak more kindly to myself.
5. To ask myself that if I had a friend who spoke to me the way I speak to myself, would I keep hanging out with them? The answer, of course, is no, so determine to be a better friend to myself.

EXAMPLE

I receive a party invitation. I remember that my automatic, conditioned self-talk will be negative because of mislabelling in my youth, I become aware of that negative self-talk and choose to speak to myself more kindly, the way I would talk to a friend.

For instance,

"My outfits are just fine, my friend Jane will be there and I enjoy her company. I always feel better once I've made an effort and I'm at the party".

TO CHALLENGE YOUR NEGATIVE SELF-TALK WILL FEEL OUT OF YOUR COMFORT ZONE AND BE DIFFICULT, EVEN SCARY, AT FIRST

Like anything worth learning, it takes practice and not just for a week or a month but for a very long time. Eventually, it will become more familiar and easier to do until it is second nature. I can say this because I have experienced it myself.

A piece of information that has helped me tremendously was from, "Mindsight", a book written by the neuroscientist and psychotherapist Daniel Siegel. He states that:

"Our thoughts and feelings are just a function of the brain. They are not objective reality".

It helped me because I had never understood why it was that it felt like my mind was working against me; that my inner dialogue remained self-critical when I was trying so hard to be well. After reading Daniel's book and in particular, this sentence, I understood that brains are made up of what they have are fed and that a brain that has been fed a diet of negative opinions during early development will mostly produce thoughts and feelings that are self-critical. His statement helped me see that these self-critical thoughts and feelings are not the objective reality of who I am and so freed me to ignore them. I had always feared my inner dialogue was the truth and that to disbelieve the self-critical thoughts was to let myself off the hook when I didn't deserve to be. Now I knew that wasn't the case.

I was finally free to be kinder to myself and change my self-talk because it was only the result of having been mislabelled by my caregivers. Over time and with a lot of determination, I changed my opinion of myself. I now participate in life with greater confidence and enjoyment. It's an ongoing journey. I continue daily to be aware of and alter my self-talk when it is negative.

And if I can do it so can you.

DON'T GIVE UP
KEEP HOPE ALIVE

GRADUALLY YOUR SELF-TALK WILL CHANGE AND YOUR LIFE WILL BE HAPPIER AND MORE FULFILLING

I recommend you keep a journal in which you record significant times you attempt to change your self-talk. Additionally, record how that helped you change your self-defeating behaviour. There will be only little changes at first. Don't be discouraged; I guarantee you that in six months you'll look back at that journal and see that you have made progress.

CHAPTER FIVE

PRACTICING GRATITUDE HELPS US MAINTAIN HOPE

This book was originally just meant to be a letter to a dear friend in response to a question she asked me. The question was:

"Karen I've seen your mental illness take you down into deep dark places. How are you able to rise out of them each time and be the positive, joyful you again? I gave up on hoping because every time I dared to hope that things could improve, my hopes were dashed. **How have you found and managed to maintain hope?".**

It was an important question with no simple answer and so the letter became a book. In the previous chapters, I've discussed important, necessary components in the building of hope but I cannot stress enough the role that gratitude plays in maintaining it.

Gratitude is vital to maintaining hope

Gratitude is not about sugar coating the experience of mental illness and playing Pollyanna with our pain. Gratitude is a tool that helps us on our journey. I know from personal experience that it is not easy to do. When we are struggling the last thing we want, or feel able, to do is be grateful. I have practised it for some years now and have found that even on days that I have had to do it through tears and gritted teeth, it has served me well. I may not have felt the effect immediately but as I have made it a daily habit, its impact has made a difference in my life.

Scientific studies are showing that practising gratitude isn't simply a way to make us "feel good". It also has a massive impact on our brain and body's internal wiring.

Some of the tested benefits are:

- It increases the amount and intensity of positive feelings you experience on a day-to-day basis.
- The positive feelings generated by gratitude immediately throw your body's natural energy into an upward spiral.
- It improves your physical health by building a stronger immune system, increasing your sleep quality and reducing aches and pains.
- It blocks negative and toxic emotions (it's impossible to feel anger and gratitude at the same time).
- It lowers anxiety and decreases the risk of clinical depression.
- It boosts confidence because you are focusing on what you have and not on what you lack.

SO HOW DO WE PRACTICE GRATITUDE?

Any habit or new skill needs to be consciously practiced each day until it becomes second nature. Therapists and wellbeing practitioners recommend you keep:

A GRATITUDE JOURNAL

It need only take 5-10 minutes of your day.

Each evening before bed, or in the morning if that suits you better, jot down 3-5 things for which you are grateful. Gratitude may not come easily at first because we become bogged down in the things that are unpleasant in our lives and in the world.

- **Be specific.** Rather than saying, "I am grateful for friends", state "I am grateful for Sarah because she cheers me up with her sense of humour", or "I am grateful for Tom because he rings me at least twice a week to see how I am".
- **Little things.** When life is hard, it's not always easy to be grateful but practicing gratitude for something as seemingly insignificant as the cup of coffee you just enjoyed, a favourite television programme, or the fact you have a roof over your head, still has a beneficial effect.
- **Take notice.** It's easy to end up repeating the same things, get bored and give up on the journal. Keep it fresh by beginning to take notice of the things around you. It could be a sunset, birdsong, or the fact that

your local supermarket delivers, so you don't have to do the chore of shopping.

Buy a notebook especially for this purpose, or if you prefer using the computer or phone, then google graceandsass.com because they offer a free online gratitude journal when you subscribe and it costs nothing to subscribe. If you don't want to write things down, it is just as useful to speak out loud the things and people for which you are grateful. It will still bring about a shift in your energy.

Remember to do this every day; even on days when you feel depressed. It will be difficult to do but it will become something you do automatically, like brushing your teeth. Set the alarm to remind you at first. Being grateful daily has a trickle-on effect and will eventually turn into a change in your sense of well-being that you will notice.

Over time practicing gratitude will change your perspective. It will lead to a more joyful outlook on life.

IT WILL HELP YOU TO MAINTAIN HOPE AS YOU PUT INTO PRACTICE WHAT YOU HAVE LEARNT IN THIS BOOK

FINAL WORDS

So, you have finished the book. That's great. I've covered several big topics and it's a lot to take in. I suggest you choose one at a time to focus on and work through. Do not become discouraged if you do not see amazing results quickly. All I've talked about in this book is a roadmap for a long journey, not directions to a nearby scenic spot for a picnic. Athletes do not give up after two weeks training because they are not winning races yet. Body builders do not quit after a month because they have not yet achieved the muscles they want. You are training; training to unlearn deeply embedded negative thought processes. You are building muscles; mind muscles.

It takes time, effort and perseverance, but I promise you, it's worth it.

I want to add here that our diagnosis is one more label we get given, only this time it is written on by a psychiatrist. The labelling is something that psychiatrists do so that they can decide what treatment to throw at us and as some of us know, they don't always get it right the first time.

Do not let this label define you.

It is not WHO you are. It merely describes a set of symptoms you have.

You are free to choose a label of your own just like my client who chose Blue Jellyfish Syndrome. I personally like Pink Flamingo syndrome.

Don't let your diagnosis own you, just make sure you are getting the help you need to stay well.

In closing, I will say:

DON'T LOSE HOPE

HOPE IS THE VITAL INGREDIENT IN THE CAKE MIX OF RECOVERY

15073635R00028

Printed in Great Britain
by Amazon